The Student's
TOOLBOX

TIPS FOR PUBLIC SPEAKING

LOUISE SPILSBURY

WAYLAND

First published in Great Britain in 2015 by Wayland

Dewey Number: 808.5'1-dc23
ISBN: 978 0 7502 9106 4
Library ebook ISBN: 978 0 7502 9107 1
10 9 8 7 6 5 4 3 2 1

MIX
Paper from
responsible sources
FSC® C104740

Wayland
An imprint of
Hachette Children's Group
Part of Hodder & Stoughton
Carmelite House
50 Victoria Embankment
London EC4Y 0DZ

An Hachette UK Company
www.hachette.co.uk

www.hachettechildrens.co.uk

Printed in China

Picture Acknowledgements:
Cover: Shutterstock: Pete Pahham. Inside: Dreamstime: Absoluteindia 14,
Anatols 19, Auremar 20, Bobsphotography 6, Dasha11 8, Deepfrog17
1, 10, Funflow 13, Joyfull 4, Kmiragaya 7, Lisafx 12, Marekuliasz 11,
Netbritish 9, Petermccue 18, Photobac 15, Pojoslaw 28, Stockyimages 17,
Yulia 22; Shutterstock: Blend Images 25, Christo 16, Goodluz 27, Robert
Kneschke 26, Mangostock 29, Milkovasa 21, Morozov67 23, Vasaleks 24,
Mikhail Zahranichny 5.

CONTENTS

WHY SPEAK WELL?

Have you ever had to stand up in front of a class and deliver a presentation? Have you listened to family members give speeches at weddings or other celebrations? Public speaking involves talking to a group of people that you know or a crowd of strangers. Public speaking is a very important part of a student's toolbox. When you know how to do it well, it can be fun, too!

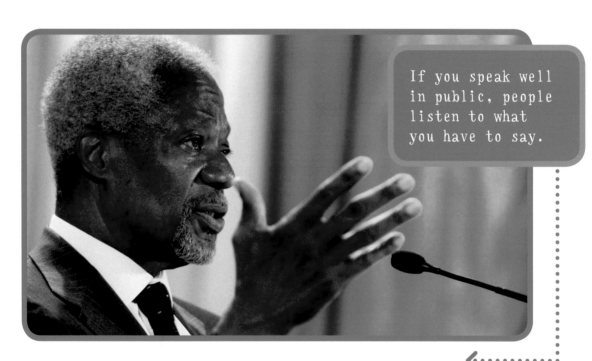

If you speak well in public, people listen to what you have to say.

A Skill for Life

To be able to speak clearly and effectively to other people is a useful skill not just for school, but for life. Public speaking is a part of many jobs, such as being a solicitor, manager, actor, teacher and tour guide. Thinking about what you say is important in your personal life, too. Working out what to say and how to make people listen to you helps you to communicate better with friends and family.

Your opinions are important so be ready to speak up!

Building Confidence

It's normal to feel nervous the first time you have to make a speech or talk in front of classmates or parents, but with practise most people start to enjoy it. If you can get used to public speaking and learn to do it well when you're young, you'll be able to take it in your stride when you have to speak in class or at work later on. Public speaking helps you in other ways, too. It helps you to:

- Develop confidence and build up your self-esteem.
- Organise your thoughts and ideas.
- Communicate information in a confident and convincing way.
- Feel a sense of achievement.

LEARN IT WELL

TIPS FOR SUCCESS

Learning to speak in front of others is a skill that is developed over time, not overnight. You can learn public speaking skills step by step, just like any other task or subject.

5

GETTING STARTED

A lot of people get nervous about public speaking because they worry about getting tongue-tied. They fear they'll get up in front of a crowd and stumble over their words. The key to successful public speaking is to get a lot of experience at talking first. Take any opportunity you can to speak up!

Start Small

Keep it simple at first. Try speaking out more when you're at home. Get into the habit of talking to your parents about your school day every day. Think about what you'll say, and turn it into a mini speech! You could read a story out loud to younger family members or ask your grandparents to be your audience. Reading aloud something that someone else has written is often easier, because you don't have to take responsibility for the words. You could also watch speeches and public performances on television and think about what the speakers do well.

Listen to other public speakers to discover how you can improve your own public speaking.

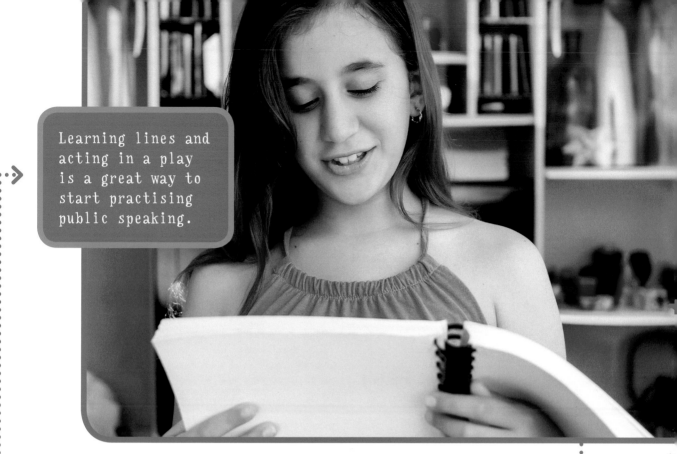

Learning lines and acting in a play is a great way to start practising public speaking.

Be Dramatic!

Another way to kick-start your public speaking skills is to do some drama. You could put on a short play for your class or family, and most schools or communities run drama clubs that you can join. You can also find out what's available in your town or city. Taking part in a show or play helps you learn things such as projecting your voice so people can hear it around an auditorium, and coping with stage fright. Doing drama is a great way to build your confidence about speaking in public because you're usually not alone on stage.

GIVE IT A TRY

Try this. Ask a parent to suggest a topic for you to speak about, without looking at any books or notes. Just speak for 30 seconds in defence of the subject, then for 30 against it. It doesn't matter what you say, it's just good practice!

TIPS FOR SUCCESS

PLANNING WHAT TO SAY

Do you think that when the prime minister stands up to make a speech, or your teacher gives a lesson, they make it up as they go along? Of course not! They need to plan what they're going to say before speaking in public, and so do you.

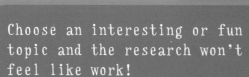
Choose an interesting or fun topic and the research won't feel like work!

Picking a Topic

If you get to choose a topic, pick one that particularly interests you, and that you want to know more about. You'll enjoy working on it, and it is more likely that you will feel confident talking about it, too. Try to choose something you already know a lot about and are comfortable talking about, such as your favourite sport or what you like to do during weekends.

The library is a good place to research your speech topic.

Research it Well

How do you know what you want to say? Facts and evidence are the heart of any speech. They can back up opinions you give in debates and explain statements in a presentation. You can research facts from websites, library books, encyclopaedias, newspapers and magazines. You can also use the world around you for research, such as interviewing local people, family and friends.

Make a Plan

Selecting a main topic is one thing, but when you have to give a long talk it's good to divide your material into subtopics. So, for example, if you have to give a talk about habitats, you might start with a general explanation of what a habitat is and then have subtopics on ocean habitats, grassland habitats, mountain habitats and so on. Grouping information in a logical way makes it easier to write a speech and easier for people to follow it.

TIPS FOR SUCCESS

BRAINSTORMING

Before you start research, you could brainstorm some ideas. Write down as many ideas as you can, without stopping, in five minutes. Try to think of some personal stories linked to your topic, as they will make your speech more interesting.

KNOW YOUR AUDIENCE

It's important to think carefully about who your audience will be when you are planning a speech. You should spend some time thinking about what they are expecting from your speech and also what will get them interested and keep them listening.

Speech Aims

Always keep in mind the main purpose of your speech. Different speeches have different jobs to do. Some speeches are simply meant to inform the audience, for example, when a teacher asks you to speak about healthy eating or the dangers of smoking. Some speeches are meant to be persuasive. That means your speech has to persuade or convince the audience to agree with you or vote for you. Other speeches need to be entertaining – for example, when you accept an award and want to include a joke.

If you smile as you make your speech, your audience is more likely to listen to you.

Speakers should pitch their speech at the right level for their audience.

Tailor Your Talk

Knowing your audience can help you plan and write your speech.

- Is the speech right for the age of your audience? If you're talking to younger children you should use simpler ideas and vocabulary than if the speech is intended for parents or the general public.

- Will the topic be interesting to the audience? If you're talking to an audience of football players, you wouldn't want to talk about tennis!

- How much does your audience already know about the topic? You want to tell them things they don't know, not repeat things they already know.

TIPS FOR SUCCESS

BE CREATIVE

Try to think of creative ways to make your speech appeal to your target audience. Think of what interests them and how you could link to those interests in your speech to make the topic more relevant to them.

11

WRITING A SPEECH

You wouldn't start out on a walk without knowing where you're going, and you shouldn't start a speech like that either! All speeches need a structure: a beginning, middle and an end. Write an outline first to plan which points to include in each part of your speech.

Make an Entrance!

In the introduction part of a speech you tell the audience what the speech is about and what main areas you will be covering. The best introductions are fairly brief but capture the audience's attention. This means you need to stamp your personality on your introduction, too. Make sure your audience knows why your speech will be important or interesting.

In the Middle

In the middle or main part of your speech, talk about the subtopics you uncovered while researching the topic. Divide it into paragraphs, with a separate paragraph for each new subtopic. If there is a time limit for your speech, work out how many paragraphs you can include. Start each with a sentence that really grabs attention.

Planning a speech carefully is essential when preparing to speak in public.

MAKE IT YOUR OWN

Write every speech in your own words. This shows that you understand the material, makes it personal and helps engage the audience. It also prevents the risk of plagiarism, which is never acceptable.

At the End

The end of your speech is the conclusion. Most speakers use the conclusion to remind listeners of the most important things they said in their speech. Like introductions, the best conclusions are brief but memorable. Try to remember the last sentence of your conclusion, so you can look at your audience when you say it. Make it snappy so the audience remembers it.

Think carefully about the focus of your speech - your conclusion should 'sum up' the core points you have made.

CHAPTER THREE

TIPS AND TECHNIQUES

People use a lot of different types of visual aids in presentations, from slides, posters and videos to puppets or even pets! Objects and images can help your audience understand your topic and hold their attention. Having visual aids can help you relax by giving you something to do with your hands as well as something to focus on.

Props can help bring a presentation to life!

Using Props

Visual aids can enhance your speeches and presentations in different ways.

- As you go through complicated parts of a speech, you can point to items on posters or overheads to help the audience follow your train of thought.

- Showing photos, illustrations or videos of something, such as a tornado, may be more effective than trying to describe in words how it looks.

- Showing facts and figures with pie charts, graphs or diagrams is more interesting than reading them as a list.

BUILD IN A BACK-UP

If a presentation relies heavily on visual aids, always have a back-up plan in case something goes wrong. For example, have some printed sheets to hand out in case your computer doesn't work or the video equipment you need isn't available.

Perfect Props

There are some important things to remember when using props and visual aids.

- Use props to highlight important points, not just for the sake of using them. Use props that really add something to the speech.

- Be sure people at the back of the auditorium will be able to see any visual aids or props you use. They are no good if people cannot see them!

- Be sure equipment is easy to use. Fiddling with buttons or displays during the speech will distract your audience.

- Be sure props are practical. Bringing in an animal might make a talk more realistic, but it might also cause a lot of problems!

Using animals as props is fun, but not ideal for a class presentation!

BODY LANGUAGE

When someone speaks to us, we don't listen just to their words. About 70 per cent of human communication is non-verbal. That means that people say more through the way they stand, how they hold their arms and their facial expressions than they ever say in words.

Posture

Your posture – the way you hold your body – can help you look interested and confident.

- Stand straight and tall. Avoid slouching; shuffling from one foot to the other; fiddling with your hands, clothes or hair; and turning your side or back to the audience.

- If there is a podium to put your notes on, try not to lean on it. This makes you look tired or bored and might make your audience tired and bored, too.

- If you walk around while giving your speech, hold your notes above your waist. Don't pace up and down too much – this could distract your listeners.

Looking nervous can make you feel more nervous, too.

EYE CONTACT

Some speakers like to look into the eyes of as many audience members as they can while they speak in order to get and keep their attention. Other speakers prefer to look at one spot or at the class teacher.

Gestures

Gestures can add something to a presentation, too. For example, you can use your hands to show how big something is or to emphasise a number – 'There are three things you need to remember about this...' To make the best use of gestures:

• Only use gestures that you would normally use in conversation. You'll feel and look awkward if you try new gestures you're not familiar or comfortable with.

• Match your facial expressions to your words. Smile if your speech is funny or has a positive message. Look sincere if the theme is more serious.

Try to use gestures and confident body language during your speech.

PREPARING TO SPEAK

You don't have to learn a whole speech by heart, but it can sound a bit dull if you just read it word for word. You can use notes written on index cards to help you deliver the speech in a more natural, conversational way.

You could write the main points of your speech on index cards.

Index Cards

You can buy index cards or cut pieces of paper or cardboard small enough to hold in your hand easily. Pick out the main points of your speech and write key words or a few notes about each of those points on separate cards. Number the cards in case they get mixed up and out of order. For example, if you're giving a talk about food chains you might use key words such as 'plants', 'make own food', 'herbivores such as zebras', 'carnivores such as lions'. Then you can glance at these words to jog your memory during your presentation.

Sleeping after reading can help you remember what you read.

Ways of Remembering

Here are some things you can do to help you remember parts of your speech.

- When you learn a section of a speech, decide exactly which gestures you want to use. Doing the gesture should help you remember the words.

- Copy the speech, or sections of it, onto a sheet of paper. Read the words aloud to yourself as you write. This can help your brain remember the script.

- Make a recording of yourself reading the speech. Listen to the recording as often as you can and try to speak along with it. Constant repetition helps us remember things.

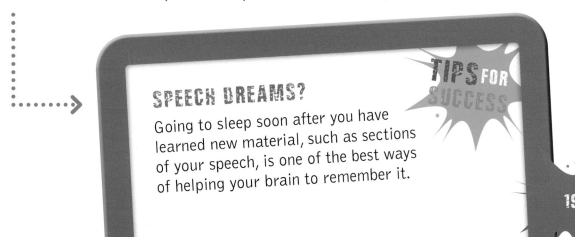

SPEECH DREAMS?

Going to sleep soon after you have learned new material, such as sections of your speech, is one of the best ways of helping your brain to remember it.

TIPS FOR SUCCESS

SPEAKING CLEARLY

When you're making a speech, a clear, confident voice will make your message more convincing and encourage people to listen more attentively. The first thing to remember is to speak up – make sure you're speaking loudly enough for everyone to hear. There are other things to remember, too.

> Speak loudly and clearly so the whole audience can hear you!

Talking Tips

When you're practising a speech, remember to:

- Speak at a medium pace, not too fast or too slow. A lot of people talk quickly when they are nervous, so take your time.

- Pronounce your words clearly, and don't slur your words. Make sure you say the ends of words, especially the *d*'s, *t*'s and *ing*'s at the ends of words.

- Don't overuse sounds such as 'Um' and 'Uh', or words such as 'you know' to fill spaces in your speech. They make you sound unprepared. Keep your cards handy and stay focused so you don't need filler words.

Sounding Natural

When you make a speech, don't try to put on a different voice. Just use your own natural voice. Use words that are familiar to you, unless you're explaining something scientific or technical. Another way to sound more natural is to use pauses and stresses. When we speak normally, we pause between phrases or add stress to key words to emphasise their meaning. For example, 'You'll never guess what happened next... (pause). She told me she just sat there and did NOTHING!'

Try some tongue twisters to help you improve your public speaking.

TONGUE TWISTERS

Tongue twisters are not just for fun! To reduce their chances of tripping over their words during a speech, or losing their place, some people practise tongue twisters. Tongue twisters exercise the face, lip and tongue muscles we use when we speak. 'She sells seashells by the seashore' is an example of a tongue twister.

TIPS FOR SUCCESS

PRACTICE MAKES PERFECT

It's an old saying but a true one: practice really does make perfect. Well, even if it doesn't make your presentation quite perfect, it'll be much better than it would have been without any practice at all! Even people who do a lot of public speaking rely on preparation and practice to make better speeches.

Take Your Time

Practise your speech as much as you can. Do it in stages.

1. Read it alone in front of a mirror until you feel more confident.

2. Read it for someone you feel comfortable with, such as a parent or friend. Ask them to stand back so they can tell if you are speaking loudly enough.

3. Record yourself so you can watch it.

4. Give and get feedback. Ask yourself and others what could be improved in terms of content and how you present the information.

Look in the mirror as you rehearse your speech.

···> Faking it

You may not feel confident about public speaking, but if you practise looking more confident you will soon feel it for real. The idea is to fake it until you make it! If you can speak calmly and clearly and remember the tips about body language, the audience won't be able to tell that you feel nervous inside, and you'll get the chance to overcome your fear through practise. Making sure you practise your talk many times beforehand helps you appear more confident too. Even if you're nervous, you will know roughly what you should say, so you can keep going no matter what.

TIME YOURSELF

When you practise your speech and you feel you are speaking at a comfortable pace, not too quickly or too slowly, use a clock or a stopwatch to time it. That way you can pace your speech to fit the time you have been given.

TIPS FOR SUCCESS

It's important to get your timing right!

WARMING UP

Everybody has butterflies in their stomach before they speak in public. A little nervous energy like this is good, because it helps you do your best. There are a lot of things you can do to help you to warm up and keep your nerves under control.

Get in the Mood

Many performers and public speakers have certain things they always do to get themselves warmed up before going on stage. Some put on their headphones and listen to their favourite song. Others get a pep talk from a parent or a friend. Others repeat a few confidence-boosting words to themselves, such as 'You can do it!' over and again.

Listening to music can relax you before a public speech.

Use Your Imagination

How good will you feel when you finish your speech and know you've done it to the best of your ability? Before you get ready to give a speech, spend a minute or two imagining that feeling. Watch a film in your mind of yourself making your speech just as well as, if not better than, all the times you've practised it. Imagine smiling confidently, listening to the applause and seeing your teacher nod with approval. Then take that feeling into the speech with you!

Breathe Deeply

Try this breathing exercise to free up your lungs to allow you to speak loudly and clearly. It will also help you feel calmer and better prepared to speak.

1. Close your mouth and breathe in deeply through your nose. Hold this breath for five seconds.

2. Then breathe out slowly through your mouth. Keep doing this until you feel calmer.

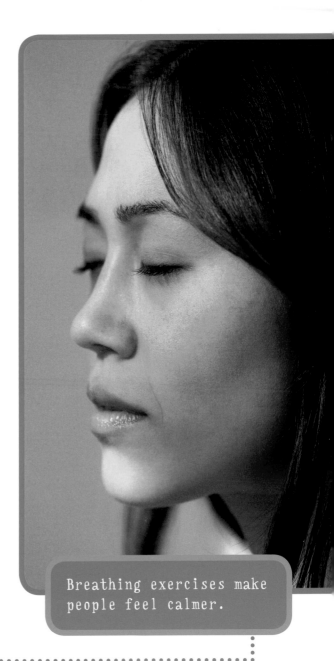

Breathing exercises make people feel calmer.

WARM UP YOUR VOICE

TIPS FOR SUCCESS

To make your voice loud and clear, warm up before you speak. Try some tongue twisters and read your speech out loud to exercise your voice.

BEING A GOOD LISTENER

Part of being a successful speaker is learning to be a good listener. If you treat what other people say as important, they will listen to you more respectfully, too. Knowing how to give helpful feedback on other people's presentations can help your own.

Listen Up!

Here are two key things to remember when listening to someone.

- Pay attention. Try not to fidget, stare out the window or talk to your neighbour. If you're distracted, it's difficult for the speaker to concentrate and you will lose the thread of the talk.

- What you have to say is important. Other people should value it. And you should value what other people have to say, too. Applaud others for their efforts when they speak in public. Most people get a little nervous, so be kind and never laugh at or make fun of a speaker.

Always be respectful and pay attention when listening to another public speaker.

Giving Feedback

It is good to know how to ask questions about something you have just heard because this helps you learn to field questions from an audience.

- If you are allowed to ask questions after someone has spoken, do it politely.

- Everyone has differing abilities, so be considerate of other people's feelings. Some people won't be able to produce as complicated a presentation as others. It's their effort that counts.

- Provide feedback in a positive way, without being rude, critical or hurtful. Don't say, 'That was awful.' Instead, say, 'That could have been even better if ...'

> Laughing with your friends during a public speech is rude - don't do it!

A GOLDEN RULE

TIPS FOR SUCCESS

When listening to other people speaking in private or in public, remember this important rule: treat other people the way you would like to be treated. For example, you wouldn't like it if someone doodled during your speech, so don't do it when someone else is speaking.

CHAPTER FOUR

ENJOY PUBLIC SPEAKING

The day of your public speaking event arrives. You've done your research, planned your talk, written your index cards, practised the words and rehearsed with the visual aids. You are ready to go. The only thing left to do is enjoy yourself!

Speak Up!

Speaking in public can be fun and incredibly satisfying. Your thoughts and opinions are important and should be heard. All you have to do is stand up, be yourself and speak with confidence. The audience's response to your speech is up to them. It's time to focus on doing your best. Be proud of yourself for speaking out.

When it is time for you to speak, take a deep breath and enjoy it.

When a speech goes well, enjoy the applause that comes your way, too!

End Well

Make the last part of your speech memorable. Maybe you could end by speaking directly to your listeners and asking them what they think about the topic you've been discussing. Or you could encourage them to take action – if you have been talking about the importance of exercise, you could suggest that they take up a new sport. If you end well, your audience is more likely to remember your speech.

Assess Yourself

After you make a presentation or speech, think back to how it went. Ask yourself some questions, such as:

- How did it feel to speak in front of a group?
- Did people respond as if they could hear everything?
- Did you keep the audience's interest?
- What could you have done better?
- When do you think you might speak in public again?

TAKING QUESTIONS

If you are well prepared you might want to end your speech by taking questions from the audience. You don't have to know all the answers. The idea is to get people involved in what you've said.

TIPS FOR SUCCESS

29

GLOSSARY

brainstorm to try to solve a problem by thinking intensely about it

communicate to exchange information or opinions with another person

concentrate to give your full attention or effort to something

conclusion the final part of an argument or text

effectively with a good result, well

encyclopaedias books that give information on many subjects or on many aspects of one subject

evidence facts and information collected to support things we say

feedback the response to information and how the information was presented

focus to concentrate and listen well

key words words with special importance or significance

opinion a personal view, idea or judgement about something

outline a general plan giving the main features but not the details

paragraphs one or more sentences written together on a single theme

pauses temporary stops in action or speech

performers people who do something in front of other people

plagiarism copying and using someone else's words for a piece of work, such as an essay

props objects used in a performance or presentation to improve an audience's understanding or enjoyment

relevant related or connected to

research investigation into something

self-esteem a sense of pride in yourself

stresses giving importance to particular words in speech or writing

structure how something is arranged

subtopics secondary topics underneath or within a main topic

technical based on precise facts

tongue twisters expressions or phrases that are difficult to say

topic a subject or theme

visual aids pictures, symbols, charts and diagrams that help to explain something that is written down or spoken

FOR MORE INFORMATION

BOOKS

CGP Books, *Key Stage 2 English The Study Book*, Coordination Group Publications, 2012

Oxford Dictionaries, *Oxford Primary Grammar, Punctuation and Spelling Dictionary*, Oxford University Press, 2013

Oxford Dictionaries, *Oxford School Dictionary*, Oxford University Press, 2012

OTHER `THE STUDENT'S TOOLBOX` BOOKS

Royston, Angela, *Tips For Better Planning*, Wayland, 2015

Spilsbury, Louise, *Tips For Better Researching*, Wayland, 2015

Spilsbury, Louise, *Tips For Better Writing*, Wayland, 2015

WEBSITES

You'll find quick and helpful tips about public speaking at:
www.wikihow.com/Overcome-Your-Fear-of-Public-Speaking

This website gives good advice on how to prepare a presentation:
http://presentationsoft.about.com/od/classrooms/tp/student_tips.htm

Visit the BBC website for great advice about how to improve your public speaking skills:
www.bbc.co.uk/speaker/improve

INDEX